Little Pebble™

Transport

Helicopters

by Mari Schuh

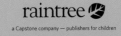

raintree

a Capstone company — publishers for children

Raintree is an imprint of Capstone Global Library Limited, a company incorporated in England and Wales
having its registered office at 264 Banbury Road, Oxford, OX2 7DY – Registered company number: 6695582

www.raintree.co.uk
myorders@raintree.co.uk

Edited by Carrie Braulick Sheely
Designed by Lori Bye
Picture research by Wanda Winch
Production by Katy LaVigne
Originated by Capstone Global Library Limited
Printed and bound in China

ISBN 978 1 4747 4433 1
21 20 19 18 17
10 9 8 7 6 5 4 3 2 1

British Library Cataloguing in Publication Data
A full catalogue record for this book is available from the British Library.

Acknowledgements
We would like to thank the following for permission to reproduce photographs: Shutterstock:
aragami12345s, cover, Art Konovalov, 5, Digital Media Pro, 17, Drew Horne, 11, Makushin Alexey, 15,
Mayskyphoto, 19, Nattapon B, 13, Nick Starichenko, 21, PixieMe, 9, Studioimagen73, 7, T. Sumaetho, zoom
motion design

Every effort has been made to contact copyright holders of material reproduced in this book. Any omissions
will be rectified in subsequent printings if notice is given to the publisher.

629.133352

Contents

On the move

Look up!

It's a helicopter!

It can fly up and down.

It can fly left and right.

It can spin.

It can hover too.

It stays in one place in the air.

Parts

Look at the rotor

blades. They spin fast.

Time to fly!

rotor blade

11

Here is the cockpit.

It has levers and pedals.

Pilots use them to fly.

pedal

lever

Look at the the skids.

A helicopter lands on them.

skids

Types

A helicopter can carry water.

It puts out fires.

A helicopter can carry cameras.

It helps to show the news.

camera

A helicopter can carry people.

Look at the big city!

Glossary

blade   one of the long, flat parts of a helicopter's rotor

cockpit   place where the pilot sits in a helicopter

hover   stay in one place in the air

lever   bar that is used to make a machine or vehicle work

pedal   flat part that you push with your foot to make a machine work

pilot   person who flies a helicopter or aeroplane

rotor   set of rotating blades that lifts an aircraft off the ground

skid   one of a pair of long narrow parts on the bottom of a helicopter or aeroplane; some helicopters land on skids

Find out more

Books

Big Machines Fly! (Big Machines), Catherine Veitch (Raintree, 2015)

Getting Around Through the Years: How Transport has Changed in Living Memory (History in Living Memory), Clare Lewis (Raintree, 2016)

Look Inside Things That Go (Usborne Look Inside) Rob Lloyd Jones (Usborne Publishing Ltd, 2013)

True or False? Transport, Dan Nunn (Raintree, 2014)

Websites

www.dkfindout.com/uk/transport/history-aircraft/helicopters/
Learn the history of helicopters.

http://www.bbc.co.uk/education/clips/zcnhgk7
Learn how a ranch in Australia uses helicopters to round up cattle.

Comprehension questions

1. How is a helicopter different from an aeroplane?

2. Name two ways that helicopters can help people.

3. What parts do helicopters use to fly?

Index